Anoint the Shield

Written by

Timothy G. Wodoslawsky

Published by

Timothy G. Wodoslawsky

Fresno, California

Fourth Edition 2019

To Teresa, Story and Valena.

Thank you for “living” this book in our family and our church. I am blessed and grateful.

Anoint the Shield

Introduction

It seems each story of the Bible contains many others. The Bible has depth like no other book. Layer upon layer of truth and wisdom is to be found by the diligent seeker. Always a main plot in plain view is supported by others that are hidden, but not less important.

The beauty of preaching is that a man can take a simple story and by the anointing of the Holy Ghost make it a profound masterpiece of God's wisdom.
How many times has each of us listened to an anointed message and thought, "I have never seen it that way before."? The main storyline was easy to see, but the underlying theme had to be revealed. That is how this book came about. It started as a preached message many years ago. Over time more (of this theme) came to light. In fact the main theme of this book came to me *while* I was preaching (not in my notes that day.) The general theme of this book is unity, and then specifically, who is responsible for maintaining that unity. This responsibility resides most with the congregation not the pastor.

I suppose good writers are akin to good preachers. They know when to stop. The length of this book is intended to be long enough to address the subject without exhausting it. It is written short enough that no one would hesitate to read it. It is a book written to reach every person.

The purpose of this book is to shed enough light for the reader to explore the depths of his or her own life. It is meant to be a torch. A torch only allows you to see so far, you must keep walking to see further. Use this torch to illuminate your life, your relationships and your church. God speed on your journey.

*All scripture quotations are from the King James Version of the Bible unless otherwise noted.

One

"The beauty of Israel is slain upon thy high places: how are the mighty fallen! Ye mountains of Gilboa, *let there be* no dew, neither *let there be* rain, upon you, nor fields of offerings: for there the shield of the mighty is vilely cast away, the shield of Saul, *as though he had* not *been* anointed with oil."

II Samuel 1:19, 21

The air was hot and thick, more so than usual. Was it humidity? All the men could feel the change in climate, but none as much as Saul. He knew it was more than weather they felt. It was judgment. His mind was rehearsing the words he heard only yesterday. "... the LORD is departed from thee and is become thine enemy." His trip to Endor had supplied the king with answers. Too many answers of the wrong nature came from that meeting. They were not the kind for which he was searching.

Suddenly the voice of his armourbearer snapped him from his mental drift, "We cannot pull back any further sir. The mount is getting too steep, the enemy will easily overtake us. They have already overtaken many at the base of the mount."

The base of the mount . . . that is where Saul had last seen his sons. Half the men had stayed while the other half abandoned their chariots and took to foot up the mount. The men at the base were to set the battle in array temporarily and then join the others in the mount. Another of his men came running to him from the base.

"My lord the Philistines number too many. They swarmed over the front line so quickly. Their advance slowed only for a moment." King Saul paused a moment as he looked down the hillside.

"My sons?", Saul asked.

The soldier hesitated awkwardly for a moment before replying, "They were at...at the forefront sire."

Saul turned to face the soldier. "Melchishua?", he asked only to receive a blank stare. "Abinadab?", he questioned again receiving the same response. "Jonathan?", came the final query.

The man's head dropped as he replied, "I am sorry, Sir."

The king paused for what seemed like an eternity, but was only a second as this news hit his ears, penetrated his mind and pierced his soul.

"Noooo!", Saul gave a bellowing cry as he threw his head back and tears began to stream down his face. His own voice seemed to blend into the one he now heard echoing in his mind from the day before. " . . . tomorrow shalt thou and thy sons be with me . . ." The climate was different today - judgment.

The sounds themselves of battle below seemed to roll up the mount in pursuit. The roaring voices of the Philistines pulled Saul into the present once again.

"Let us make it to the tree line. The forest will help protect us from the archers. We will hold our position there." Saul had barely finished speaking when a barrage of arrows dropped all around them, and then another.

"Make haste!", he yelled.

He raised his shield as a third wave of arrows whistled in. This time one found its mark. The arrow hit Saul's shield, but rather than being deflected, it burst through the hide and pierced him deeply. It pierced so deep his mind swam with pain...and remorse.

Saul crumpled to the earth in agony. The arrow went through the ribs into the lung, the color red was already showing on his lips.

"Draw your sword and thrust me through. Finish me before these uncircumcised come to do it and abuse me.", he commanded weakly.

His armourbearer stood there dumbfounded and motionless.

"Do it man!", Saul gasped.

Still no movement. The king yet had a firm grasp upon the shield that had failed him. With disgust he cast it aside. Saul gathered his strength as he rose to his feet, pulled his own sword from its scabbard, firmly planted the hilt into the ground between some stones and as he steadied the blade with both hands he lunged upon its tip.

"So Saul died..." - I Samuel 31:6

The story of Saul is one of the great heartbreaks found in scripture. Samuel's heart was broken. David's heart was broken and no doubt so was the Lord's. A man with so much promise and potential finishes as a tragedy. There is much to be learned from all of Saul's life. However, this book starts with one verse pertaining to his story which seemingly has little significance. It is the one verse about Saul's shield.

The shield - this was a vital piece of battle gear. It provided the necessary balance between good offense and good defense. Proper care for the condition of a sword was important. Maintaining proper care for the condition of the shield was no less important and perhaps more so. It certainly seems so for Saul this day.

To see what happened to Saul we must look at these verses again.

"The beauty of Israel is slain upon thy high places: how are the mighty fallen! Ye mountains of Gilboa, *let there be* no dew, neither *let there be* rain, upon you, nor fields of offerings: for there the shield of the mighty is vilely cast away, the shield of Saul, *as though he had* not *been* anointed with oil." (II Samuel 1:19, 21)

The King James translators did a tremendous job of giving us the best word for word translation of the scriptures. When the translators felt the need of adding words to help the flow of the verse these words were identified. Today we see words that were added designated by *italics*. Read these verses again with the italics removed.

"The beauty of Israel is slain upon thy high places: how are the mighty fallen! Ye mountains of Gilboa, no dew, neither rain, upon you, nor fields of offerings: for there **the shield** of the mighty is vilely cast away, **the shield** of Saul, **not anointed with oil**." (II Samuel 1:19, 21)

Removing the italics does not usually affect the meaning of the verse. However, this is one of the rare occasions where it does. The translators predominantly did an outstanding work, but remember they were just men and translating from language to language does have its difficulties. To further prove the point look at two other translations of these verses.

"Thy glory, O Israel, is slain upon thy high places! How are the mighty fallen! Ye mountains of Gilboa, Let there be no dew nor rain upon you, neither fields of offerings: For there the shield of the mighty was vilely cast away, The shield of Saul, **not anointed with oil**." (II Samuel 1:19, 21 – ASV)

"Your glory, O Israel, lies slain on your heights. How the mighty have fallen! "O mountains of Gilboa, may you have neither dew nor rain, nor fields that yield offerings of grain. For there the shield of the mighty was defiled, the shield of Saul--**no longer rubbed with oil**." (II Samuel 1:19, 21 – NIV)

The focus of verse 21 is upon Saul's shield not Saul. The American Standard Version says "not anointed with oil" and the New International Version says "no longer rubbed with oil". Other English versions portray this same connotation of an anointing on the shield. Anointing shields was a common practice. Here is another verse addressing this.

"Prepare the table, watch in the watchtower, eat, drink: arise, ye princes, and **anoint the shield**." (Isaiah 21:5)

Not all shields were made of metal as one might think. Many shields were made of leather stretched over a frame. The leather shields were lighter and easier to handle. If properly cared for, these shields provided good defense for deflecting blows from the enemy.

Leather will not retain its resiliency naturally. It will dry out and crack. Leather must be treated in order to maintain flexibility and strength. Perhaps the reader has done this with a new baseball glove. Oil is rubbed into a new glove to promote flexibility and longevity. Trying to catch with a brand new glove can be difficult. A glove that has been "worked" is a useful tool for the game.

The same was true for these shields. These were rubbed or "anointed" with oil. This anointing provided for protection in the day of battle. Certainly Saul failed to ensure his equipment was battle ready.

This is a reflection of much of his life. However, who else was responsible?

Two

Saul's armourbearer stood motionless. The last few minutes had both raced and crawled by. Now he stood staring at the lifeless body of his king. He must flee, but his feet seemed immovable.

He looked at the shield Saul had cast away. A gaping hole in the top right side was where the enemy's blow entered. He looked back at the king and then at the shield once more. He swallowed hard. His negligence caused Saul's shield to fail. All of the king's armour was entrusted to his care.

"Run you fool!" These words seemed to explode in his mind. If he could escape, surely the new king, David, would route the Philistines. David . . . now the armourbearer could hear a voice from his past. It was the day before he was promoted to be at the side of Saul. . .

"Abner. Abner. Will you not answer, Abner?", the voice of David came down from the hilltop in the stillness of the night.

"Who are you that cries out to the king?", replied Abner.

David cried out the more, "I am not calling out to the King, I am calling out to you. Are you not a valiant man? Who is like you in all of Israel? Why have you not kept your lord the king? One of the people came in tonight to kill the king, your lord. What you have done is not good. As the LORD lives, you are worthy of death, because you have not kept watch over your master, the LORD's anointed. Now look where the king's spear is and his water that sat at his head." David raised a spear and a cruse of water into the light of a torch.

"Death to the host of Israel!", the voices of the Philistines were getting closer. Even if he lived past the day, once David discovered how Saul died, which he surely would, life would be over. He was a dead man either way. The armourbearer mirrored his master. He drew his sword, set it firmly and joined his king.

"So Saul died, and his three sons, and his armourbearer . . ." - I Samuel 31:6

Undoubtedly Saul should have monitored the care and condition of his battle equipment. After all it was his life that depended upon these items. Inspecting these items to be sure of their integrity was the responsibility of the user. However, the responsibility of maintaining their integrity rested squarely on the shoulders of the armourbearer.

What is an armourbearer? This Bible word is derived from two Hebrew words: *Nasa* – Strong's number 5375 and *Keliy* number 3627. These two words together give us the English word. Together we have a word that means *to bear, carry, support, sustain, aid, assist* specifically *implements of war*. The shield is included.

Who needs an armourbearer? Biblically it seems anyone in a leadership position. Not only did the king have an armourbearer, but others did also. Here are some other examples in scripture of men and their armourbearers.

The book of II Samuel lists David's mighty men. There are 37 men named. In this list we see one of them is Joab's armourbearer. " . . . Nahari the Beerothite, armourbearer to Joab the son of Zeruiah . . ." – (II Samuel 23:37).

Joab is a prominent figure throughout the life of David. An inventory of David's mighty men reveals three men associated with Joab. Two of them were his brothers, Asahel and Abishai. The other is his armourbearer, Nahari. The amazing thing about this is that Joab is not on the list of David's mighty men, but his armourbearer is.

Jonathan, King Saul's son, had an armourbearer. I Samuel 14:4-14 tells of these men fighting together against the Philistines. "And his armourbearer said unto him, Do all that is in thine heart: turn thee; behold, I am with thee according to thy heart. . . . And Jonathan climbed up upon his hands and upon his feet, and his armourbearer after him: and they fell before Jonathan; and his armourbearer slew after him." – Verses seven and fourteen give us a glimpse of the attitude of an armourbearer. This man followed the lead of Jonathan and together they won a great victory.

One of the most famous stories from the Bible is that of David and Goliath. Within the account of this battle between these two characters there is a third mentioned. "And the Philistine came on and drew near unto David; and the man that bare the shield went before him." – (I Samuel 17:41). Even Goliath had an armourbearer. The implication of this is that no matter how BIG or "bad" someone is, they still need an armourbearer.

In these references one can see that not only does the armourbearer care for the equipment, but also battles with and for his leader (and his people). One was a mighty man, one fought with Jonathan and one bear the shield before Goliath. This position has multiple and great responsibilities. It is not an easy role to fulfill. In the time we live, the time of the New Covenant in God's Kingdom, there are still armourbearers. There is a tremendous need for individuals to step into this role. As we shall see it should be regarded as a high calling.

Three

The fugitive stepped from his hiding place to the end of the small ledge. His eyes burned as tears streamed across his face. His voice cracked as he cried out, "My lord, the king!"

Saul turned in the direction of the voice. As he did David dropped to his knees and bowed his face to the earth. He lifted up, still on his knees. Mud from his sweat, tears and the dirt stuck to his forehead and the bridge of his nose. Both hands were raised. One hand was empty, in the other the skirt of a robe was clenched.

His chest was heaving with emotion as he spoke again, "Why do you listen to those who say, David seeks to do you great harm?" Behold, this day with your very own eyes you see how in this cave the LORD put you into my hands. Some of my men wanted me to kill you, but I wouldn't do it. I told them that I won't lift my hand against my master, because he is the LORD's anointed."

David shook the garment in his hand. "Oh, my father, look at this, look at the skirt of your robe here in my hand. I cut your robe, I could have cut you – killed you, but I didn't. I am not against you, look at the evidence!"

David paused shaking the garment again. "I haven't sinned against you, yet you are still hunting to kill me. The LORD may judge us, and the LORD may avenge me of you, but it is in his hands, not mine. The ancient proverb says, "Wickedness comes from the wicked." So be assured that my hand will not be upon you. Who has the king of Israel come out to pursue? – I am a dead dog, a flea. Therefore let the LORD judge us, plead my cause and deliver me out of your hand." His hands came down to rest upon his knees and his head dropped.

The voice and tears of David pushed the fog and torment from the mind of Saul. The reality of what had just happened shook him to the soul. The king for a brief moment was able to reason with clarity.

"Is that the voice of my son, David?", he responded. He also was now weeping and sobbing. "You are far better than I am, you have rewarded my evil with good. God placed me into your hands, but you did not kill me. If a man finds his enemy will he let him go? May the LORD reward you for the kindness you have shown me this day. I know that you will be king and the kingdom of Israel will be established in your hand. Promise me before the LORD, that you will not kill off my family or wipe out my name."

David promised.

I Samuel 16 (adapted from KJV and The Message)

David may be the most referenced Old Testament character and for good reason. He is an excellent example to use for many aspects of life. This story shows one of them. That is his faithfulness. David loved the Lord's kingdom, the Lord's people and the Lord's anointed more than he loved himself. Even though David had to flee in order to preserve his own life, his flight did not negate his loyalty to the king. David is the picture of a model armourbearer.

"But the Spirit of the LORD departed from

Saul, and an evil spirit from the LORD troubled him. And Saul's servants said unto him, Behold now, an evil spirit from God troubleth thee. Let our lord now command thy servants, which are before thee, to seek out a man, who is a cunning player on an harp: and it shall come to pass, when the evil spirit from God is upon thee, that he shall play with his hand, and thou shalt be well. And Saul said unto his servants, Provide me now a man that can play well, and bring him to me. Then answered one of the servants, and said, Behold, I have seen a son of Jesse the Bethlehemite, that is cunning in playing, and a mighty valiant man, and a man of war, and prudent in matters, and a comely person, and the LORD is with him. Wherefore Saul sent messengers unto Jesse, and said, Send me David thy son, which is with the sheep. And David came to Saul, and stood before him: and he loved him greatly; and **he became his armourbearer**." (I Samuel 16:14- 19, 21)

This setting of scripture is immediately after Samuel anoints David to become king. David goes back to tending sheep. Unexpectedly he is called to come before Saul. Apparently David already had quite a reputation in the land. That reputation reached all the way into the king's palace. How his family perceived him was not how others did. Even before his victory over Goliath, David was known not only as a cunning player of the harp, but also as a man who was mighty, valiant and prudent. His character paved the way for his entrance into the king's house and his position with Saul. Long before David was ever a king he was an armourbearer. It seems that David would have been content to remain an armourbearer indefinitely. Throughout his life he did not seek his own glory.

"Let nothing be done through strife or vainglory; but in lowliness of mind let each esteem other better than themselves. Look not every man on his own things, but every man also on the things of others." (Philippians 2:3, 4)

This was written hundreds of years after David, yet he lived this verse. He deferred honor to the king and remained faithful. (Even during Absalom's rebellion he fled. His thought was that maybe the overthrow was of the Lord and his time as king was finished. If not God would restore the kingdom back to David. – II Samuel 15:25, 26)

Perhaps no one loved Saul as much as David did. He always demonstrated that he was for the king not against him. Until the end of Saul's life David remained this way and even then he was the same. He was the one who made a great lamentation at Saul's death (II Samuel 1). David was a man of incredible character and one to look to as an example, no matter what our place is in God's kingdom today.

Four

"Finally, my brethren, be strong in the Lord, and in the power of his might. Put on the whole armour of God, that ye may be able to stand against the wiles of the devil. For we wrestle not against flesh and blood, but against principalities, against powers, against the rulers of the darkness of this world, against spiritual wickedness in high places. Wherefore take unto you the whole armour of God, that ye may be able to withstand in the evil day, and having done all, to stand. Stand therefore, having your loins girt about with truth, and having on the breastplate of righteousness; And your feet shod with the preparation of the gospel of peace; **Above all, taking the shield of faith**, wherewith ye shall be able to quench all the fiery darts of the wicked. And take the helmet of salvation, and the sword of the Spirit, which is the word of God: Praying always with all prayer and supplication in the Spirit, and watching thereunto with all perseverance and supplication for all saints;" (Ephesians 6:10-18)

Here is the New Testament shield. Strong's Exhaustive Concordance identifies **faith** in this verse as the Greek word *pistis* (4102) which means – fidelity, loyalty, faithfulness.

Fidelity in the Mirriam-Webster Thesaurus has quite a description for its understanding. It is "constancy to something to which one is bound by a pledge or duty." The synonyms listed are – allegiance, ardor, devotion, faithfulness, fealty, loyalty, piety, constancy, staunchness, steadfastness, dependability, reliability, trustworthiness.

"Let a man so account of us, as of the ministers of Christ, and stewards of the mysteries of God. Moreover it is required in stewards, that a man be found faithful." (I Corinthians 4:1, 2)

Fidelity, loyalty, faithfulness – this is the shield that protects a child of God. On a personal level it protects the individual and the family. On a kingdom level it protects the church and the man of God. This is a most powerful part of the armour of God. It is so much so that the writer was inspired by God to write the words "Above all" as a preface to taking up the shield. The Lord is the master communicator. If he begins a thought with **above all** we should pay close attention to what follows.

The shield of fidelity – loyalty – faithfulness requires maintenance. Even the most faithful person must work on the condition of this trait. It is not always easily kept in a pristine state. We must keep it anointed. When kept in good condition, this shield will stand the test of time and trials.

Where does this anointing come from? Of

course it comes from God. What is the anointing? The word of God provides the answer.

"Behold, how good and how pleasant it is for brethren to dwell together in unity! It is like the precious ointment upon the head, that ran down upon the beard, even Aaron's beard: that went down to the skirts of his garments; As the dew of Hermon, and as the dew that descended upon the mountains of Zion: for there the LORD commanded the blessing, even life for evermore." (Psalm 133:1-3)

This scripture likens the anointing upon Aaron to unity. There are many examples of anointing in the scriptures. It is significant that this particular anointing upon Aaron was chosen as a parallel to unity. This will be examined later. Let it suffice for now that the Lord views unity as a special anointing.

"I therefore, the prisoner of the Lord, beseech you that ye walk worthy of the vocation wherewith ye are called, With all lowliness and meekness, with longsuffering, forbearing one another in love; **Endeavouring to keep the unity of the Spirit** in the bond of peace." (Ephesians 4:1-3)

The New Testament writers place great emphasis upon unity. Notice that we are to endeavor to **keep** the unity of the Spirit. That means the unity is already there. It was established by God. If there is disunity it is not the Lord's doing. It is a result of man's carnality.

"For all the law is fulfilled in one word, even in this; Thou shalt love thy neighbour as thyself. But if ye bite and devour one another, take heed that ye be not consumed one of another. This I say then, Walk in the Spirit, and ye shall not fulfil the lust of the flesh. For the flesh lusteth against the Spirit, and the Spirit against the flesh: and these are **contrary** the one to the other: so that ye cannot do the things that ye would." (Galatians 5:14-17)

We see that the unity is put in place by the Spirit of God. It is obvious, however, that it takes work to maintain that unity. Our carnal nature is going to oppose the Spirit of unity. The Spirit and the flesh are in conflict.

"Put on therefore, as the elect of God, holy and beloved, bowels of mercies, kindness, humbleness of mind, meekness, longsuffering; Forbearing one another, and forgiving one another, if any man have a quarrel against any: even as Christ forgave you, so also do ye. And above all these things **put on charity, which is the bond of perfectness**." (Colossians 3:12-14)

"So, as those who have been chosen of God, holy and beloved, put on a heart of compassion, kindness, humility, gentleness and patience; bearing with one another, and forgiving each other, whoever has a complaint against anyone; just as the Lord forgave you, so also should you. Beyond all these things **put on love, which is the perfect bond of unity**." (Colossians 3:12-14 NASB)

Charity – unselfish love, this is the perfect bond of unity. It brings the needed anointing. Unifying love keeps us loyal and faithful. It keeps us loyal/faithful to God, to one another (the church) and to the man of God. It binds us together. Without it loyalty dries up. Faithfulness cracks. Fidelity shatters. The shield fails.

"Let us not be desirous of vain glory, provoking one another, envying one another." (Galatians 5:26)

"If there be therefore any consolation in Christ, if any comfort of love, if any fellowship of the Spirit, if any bowels and mercies, **Fulfil ye my joy, that ye be likeminded, having the same love, being of one accord, of one mind**. Let nothing be done through strife or vainglory; but in lowliness of mind let each esteem other better than themselves. Look not every man on his own things, but every man also on the things of others." (Philippians 2:1-4)

This same thought the Apostle Paul writes to the saints in Galatia, Colosse and Philippi. That is to have our focus on others not ourselves. That is true charity – love. This is what <u>keeps</u> the anointing of unity. These verses are pointing us in the direction of what the Lord is looking for in and from his church. What kind of unity does the Lord desire? Read the words of Jesus himself. His prayer recorded in John chapter 17 tells us.

"Sanctify them through thy truth: thy word is truth. As thou hast sent me into the world, even so have I also sent them into the world. And for their sakes I sanctify myself, that they also might be sanctified through the truth. Neither pray I for these alone, but for them also which shall believe on me through their word; That they all may be one; as thou, Father, art in me, and I in thee, that they also may be one in us: that the world may believe that thou hast sent me. And the glory which thou gavest me I have given them; **that they may be one, even as we are one**: I in them, and thou in me, that they may be made perfect in one; and that the world may know that thou hast sent me, and hast loved them, as thou hast loved me." (John 17:17-23)

There is no greater picture of unity than the Godhead. He wants his people to have that same unity. This is God's desire for his people with each other and with him. According to Psalm 133 this is where God **commands** the blessing. If God is commanding a blessing somewhere, that is where each of us should desire to be.

In order to be in that place of unity where God commands the blessing we have a battle on our hands. We must battle against pride. We must battle against our own selfish desires. Even desires that are not self serving, but for the furtherance of the kingdom must be brought in subjection to be in unity with God's timing. Our will must align with God's will.

This battle is not just against our carnal nature. In fact our carnal nature is really only a tool of our real enemy. The enemy of God and God's people has been causing disruptions in unity from the beginning. The founder of division, Satan, is going to do all he can to disrupt unity.

Five

Colors flashed synchronous with the music. The full spectrum of light danced in every direction. The music was a symphony. If mortal ears could have heard it, waves of emotion would have rolled causing tears, laughter, joy, reverence all at once. Words could not describe this melody of praise. It truly was heavenly.

Gemstones sparkling, glistening, dazzling, reflecting the glory of God with the turn of every facet. The sounds of a thousand instruments filled Heaven. The orchestration of this cherub seemed to stream to the other cherubim as they flew and spun through the lights. The flashing of light bouncing from the iridescence of their wings and vestures was an incredible sight of its own.

The music of the anointed cherub flowed over his

fellow creatures and they burst into song. These sons of God united in perfect harmony to bring praise and honor to their Creator.

"Son of man, take up a lamentation upon the king of Tyrus, and say unto him, Thus saith the Lord GOD; Thou sealest up the sum, full of wisdom, and perfect in beauty. Thou hast been in Eden the garden of God; every precious stone was thy covering, the sardius, topaz, and the diamond, the beryl, the onyx, and the jasper, the sapphire, the emerald, and the carbuncle, and gold: the workmanship of thy tabrets and of thy pipes was prepared in thee in the day that thou wast created. Thou art the anointed cherub that covereth; and I have set thee so: thou wast upon the holy mountain of God; thou hast walked up and down in the midst of the stones of fire. Thou wast perfect in thy ways from the day that thou wast created, till iniquity was found in thee." (Ezekiel 28:12-15)

"How art thou fallen from heaven, O Lucifer, son of the morning! how art thou cut down to the ground, which didst weaken the nations! For thou hast said in thine heart, I will ascend into heaven, I will exalt my throne above the stars of God: I will sit also upon the mount of the congregation, in the sides of the north: I will ascend above the heights of the clouds; I will be like the most High." (Isaiah 14:12-14)

The scripture does not give us an extreme amount of detail about this Bible character. Different portions have been pieced together to provide us with what we believe happened. God does not spend much time addressing this and neither will this book. It is this writer's understanding, that the most common explanation is that Lucifer was God's first worship leader. Simply put, somehow pride got into Lucifer and he led a rebellion against his Creator. He and one third of the host of Heaven fell. There was unity in Heaven and he brought division.

God said that Lucifer was full of wisdom and perfect in beauty. Precious stones were built into his covering. Music was a part of his being. He was designed and created for a specific purpose. Notice that Lucifer was the **anointed** cherub. That anointing was to bring glory to God. I believe that this anointing was more than that. The anointing was also to unify the host of heaven in their honoring the creator. The anointing put him in a position of influence which he used honorably and perfectly until he sinned.

This is the beginning and source of disunity. The division which he started in heaven was brought to earth, specifically to the garden. Here the target for disunity was Eve. Take note that Satan's focus was not upon the primary leader (Adam). He has followed this pattern of creating disunity ever since. His focus for bringing division is almost always upon an individual who has influence, but is not the primary or main leader.

Six

Bursts of lightning in the midst of the vapor and smoke accented each syllable. The voice of God thundered in the mount, "Get down from the mount for the people have corrupted themselves." Moses trembled as the words of the LORD continued.

Joshua gazed toward the mount where he had seen Moses disappear. He could not hear the words, but he could feel their power. Something had changed. It wasn't for the good.

Moses rushed down the side of the mount towards Joshua. Joshua was now looking toward the camp as Moses came up behind him. As the elder passed Joshua said, "There is the sound of war in the camp." He hurried to catch up to Moses.

"That is not the shout of victory or defeat, but it is singing I hear.", Moses said heatedly, stuttering more than usual as he quickened his pace. He was clutching two tables of stone, one in each hand. Joshua followed silent and perplexed.

Moses entered the camp. He approached a large circle of people dancing and singing. As he did many noticed his arrival and the circle opened to make way. He marched to the center of the circle and when he saw the golden calf his anger left him speechless. He cast the two stone tablets to the earth shattering them. The camp fell silent as the old man's eyes filled with fire scanned the crowd until they rested upon his brother.

Notice that the anointing found in Psalm 133 was upon Aaron and not Moses. **The anointing to promote unity is not given to the primary leader; this special anointing is upon second and third level leaders and beyond**. Please read that sentence again and allow it to sink in because this thought is the focal point of this book – who is responsible to keep unity intact.

Moses was the prophet, Aaron was the high priest. Was Aaron a leader? There is no doubt he was, but he was not the primary leader. He had a subordinate position of authority. However, he still had authority and even more important he had influence. He was in a place with a delicate balance of leading and following. This put him in a place of great responsibility.

Aaron's anointing was likened with unity in Psalm 133. So it could be said that he was anointed not just as the high priest and leader of the worship system within the tabernacle, but also to maintain the unity of the people behind the leadership of Moses.

For whatever reason, God parallels the worship system of Heaven where Lucifer was the leader with that of the Tabernacle and Aaron. Lucifer was the anointed cherub – Aaron was the anointed high priest. All of the precious stones found in Lucifer's covering are found in Aaron's. Music and instruments were "prepared" in Lucifer and there were bells and dried pomegranates attached to the bottom of Aaron's vesture. It seems throughout man's history God has put people in positions to succeed where Lucifer failed.

Aaron had failed in this capacity in the beginning of Israel's time at Sinai. Unfortunately he and Miriam speak against Moses in Numbers chapter twelve because of Moses' Ethiopian wife.

The judgment of God came with leprosy upon Miriam. Aaron beseeches Moses for mercy and Moses intercedes before God on their behalf.

It seems after these two incidents Aaron does not fail in this way again. The problem of disunity did not stop with Aaron. It went further down the leadership line and into the congregation. In Numbers chapter sixteen we read about Korah, Dathan and Abiram along with 250 princes of the assembly. These were famous in the congregation and men of renown. Notice again these are second and third level leaders. These men began saying that Moses and Aaron take too much upon themselves and that all the congregation are holy. What happens next? The judgment of God comes.

Before all of this Israel had trouble from the time they left Egypt. The twelve spies that were first sent into the Promised Land were leaders from their tribes. We cannot read about the conversation on the way back from Canaan to the camp of Israel, but we can use our imagination. No doubt there was already an animated discussion taking place about deviating from God's plan as delivered by Moses. Ten second level leaders turned the hearts of virtually the entire host of Israel away from the direction of the primary leader, Moses. Their responsibility was to keep the unity. Instead they brought division.

The Bible is replete with examples. The point is not failure and judgment. The point is to take note of **where** the failure occurred, learn from it and adjust our own life. All these things are written as examples. Read the Apostle Paul's explanation of Israel's record.

"Moreover, brethren, I would not that ye should be ignorant, how that all our fathers were under the cloud, and all passed through the sea; And were all baptized unto Moses in the cloud and in the sea; And did all eat the same spiritual meat; And did all drink the same spiritual drink: for they drank of that spiritual Rock that followed them: and that Rock was Christ. But with many of them God was not well pleased: for they were overthrown in the wilderness. Now these things were our examples, to the intent we should not lust after evil things, as they also lusted. Neither be ye idolaters, as were some of them; as it is written, The people sat down to eat and drink, and rose up to play. Neither let us commit fornication, as some of them committed, and fell in one day three and twenty thousand. Neither let us tempt Christ, as some of them also tempted, and were destroyed of serpents. Neither murmur ye, as some of them also murmured, and were destroyed of the destroyer. **Now all these things happened unto them for examples: and they are written for our admonition**, upon whom the ends of the world are come. Wherefore let him that thinketh he standeth take heed lest he fall." (I Corinthians 10:1- 12)

Each of us needs to take heed. Anyone can fall into the trap of the great "divider". Division is what Satan uses to conquer. Thank God we are "more than conquerors" through him who loved us by the power of the Holy Ghost!

Consider the term – primary leader. The reason I use this term is because this concept stretches beyond the pastor / saint relationship. Understanding this idea of primary, secondary (and beyond) leaders in regard to other areas will help us understand it within the church.

The responsibility to maintain unity touches every part of life. The wife, not the husband, has the primary influence to keep unity in the home. Students, not teachers, are responsible in the classroom. Employees, not owners, are responsible in business. Staff, not department heads, are responsible within organizations. Players, not coaches, are responsible on teams. **Saints in the pew, not pastors in the pulpit, are responsible within the church**. In every group structure this concept holds true.

The Apostle Paul wrote the charge to endeavor to "keep the unity of the Spirit" to saints not to pastors. It was written "to the saints which are at Ephesus" not to Timothy or Titus or Philemon. God makes no mistakes; this was written to the right group.

Though the challenge of maintaining unity never ceases, the challenge is never upon God's lead man, it is always upon those who follow and support him. The paradox of the primary leader is that this person can do much to disrupt unity and little to maintain it. The second, third level leaders and beyond have more influence for both disruption and preservation.

How many tragic stories are there in which the shield (of faithfulness) lost the anointing (of unity) and failed? There are too many examples of an assistant within a church whose influence was abused and became a major contributor to a split, a church board that had their own agenda and resisted the leadership of the pastor. Perhaps it was just an uprising of the "saints" against God's man. The role of the armourbearer was abandoned. The unity was not "kept" and the shield of protection failed and was cast away.

Fortunately there are many churches that keep the unity in the bond of peace. The pastor is able to promote a climate of love and brotherhood. More importantly the people, from the leadership into the congregation, maintain that climate. Even if there is one or a few that are divisive the overall atmosphere is unaffected. This should be the goal of every saint in every congregation – a church where love abounds anointed by unity and shielded by faithfulness.

Seven

The final edge of the sun slipped below the horizon. The golden glow in the sky dimly lit the city below – Nazareth. Soon he would be headed home. He sat on a large rock to overlook the city. To his right there was a small pile of stones round and smooth. This wasn't the first time he had seen them. It was the first time he noticed that they looked much like his mother's homemade bread. Possibly it was the lighting. Maybe it was the pangs of hunger setting in. It had been weeks since he even felt hungry. Now that feeling had returned and was getting stronger.

He could sense an approach behind him. It wasn't swift, but gradual. He didn't bother to turn and look. He recognized this presence. It felt different in a body of flesh, but still unmistakable. A shadow darker than those from the twilight eased next to him.

The Lord spoke first, "I knew you would come. I have been waiting for you." He said this with calm confidence. His eyes remained fixed upon the pile of stones.

That assertion seemed to create a hesitation. Then the Lord could sense that his visitor was emboldened by the veiled challenge. A dark voice spoke, "If you are the Son of God, command that these stones be made bread."

The Lord had to force himself not to smirk. He had anticipated this day for a long time. This was the beginning of reconciling the failure in Eden. He turned to face his adversary.

Boldness and power coursed through him as he began his response, "It is written..."

"There hath no temptation taken you but such as is common to man:" (I Corinthians 10:13)

"Seeing then that we have a great high priest, that is passed into the heavens, Jesus the Son of God, let us hold fast our profession. For we have not an high priest which cannot be touched with the feeling of our infirmities; but was in all points tempted like as we are, yet without sin." (Hebrews 4:14, 15)

From the wilderness to the garden and then to the cross there was the constant battle for the Son of God to remain faithful to the Father and his plan. "Great is the mystery of Godliness" (I Timothy 3:16), the manifestation of God (the Father) in the form of a man (the son). We may not fully comprehend this mystery. How did God humble himself and take on the form of a servant (a man) and become obedient? The Apostle Paul tells us "God was in Christ" (II Corinthians 5:19) and "in him dwelleth all the fullness of the Godhead bodily" (Colossians 2:9). Completely man. Completely God. Never-the-less there are important lessons for us, who are only "man", to learn in this mystery. It appears there was a constant battle even for Jesus Christ between the weakness of the flesh and the willingness/strength of the spirit.

Jesus stood yet on the mountain. Satan had departed and so had the angels. The vision of the kingdoms of the world lingered in the Lord's mind. Love burned in his heart for the people in those kingdoms.

This encounter seemed anti-climactic, almost too easy. He knew not all the tests would be this way. Presently he felt no clash of the will. However, there was an end for which he was born. He knew that in that "end" the wills would collide. He was not sure how or when, but there would be a battle of the wills before that end came.

"And he went a little farther, and fell on his face, and prayed, saying, O my Father, if it be possible, let this cup pass from me: nevertheless <u>not as I will, but as thou wilt</u>." (Matthew 26:39)

In chapter 4 of this book we looked at a principle found in Philippians 2:1-4. That is to have our focus on others not ourselves – humility. See here how that setting of scripture continues.

"Let this mind be in you, which was also in Christ Jesus: Who, being in the form of God, thought it not robbery to be equal with God: But made himself of no reputation, and took upon him the form of a servant, and was made in the likeness of men: And being found in fashion as a man, he humbled himself, and became obedient unto death, even the death of the cross." (Philippians 2:5-8)

Unity requires a significant component: a progression of authority, submission and obedience. *Where true Christian love abounds there is neither the abuse of authority nor the lack of submission.*

Once again, “charity is the bond of perfectness” and charity is what binds these two critical elements (authority and submission) of unity together.

Since Jesus is the “author and finisher of our faith” (Hebrews 12:2) and our ultimate example for life, he must provide us a pattern to follow for this also, which of course he does. The son (humanity) had to submit to the eternal will of the Father (Spirit) in order to maintain the unity of God’s purpose and plan. The temptation to deviate from the purpose of his presence in the earth confronted the Lord many times and ways, yet he remained faithful to the will of God.

“But that the world may know that I love the Father; and as the Father gave me commandment, even so I do.” (John 14:31)

Jesus taught his disciples these principles by word and example. When they disputed amongst themselves about who was greatest the Lord presented them with a child for a lesson (Matthew 18). When the Lord spoke to them about his soon to come suffering and death, Peter rebuked him. Read the Lord’s reply in Matthew chapter sixteen.

“But he turned, and said unto Peter, Get thee behind me, Satan: thou art an offence unto me: for thou savourest not the things that be of God, but those that be of men. Then said Jesus unto his disciples, If any man will come after me, let him deny himself, and take up his cross, and follow me." (Matthew 16:23, 24)

In the end Jesus washed his disciples' feet. The child taught humility. The rebuke taught submission. The washing taught servitude. Scripture and experience continue to teach us to this day that the battle for unity and faithfulness goes on and is fought in the forefront of these principles.

Every Christian and every church will battle disunity. It is common to all man. This is not unique to one location, one church, or one person. Because we are individuals we are different and we will have differences of opinion. Unity is not agreement in respect of a point of view. In that we will not always agree, but we can still have agreement in the sense of harmony. When there is "anointed" authority and submission there will still be unity. Disagreement does not have to lead to division. Understanding that unity brings God's blessing should motivate its pursuit.

Our great example of unity for the church begins in Acts chapter two. Notice when the day of Pentecost was fully come, they were all with one accord (unity) in one place. Suddenly the blessing came, even life for evermore. We need another day of unity to fully come into our churches.

Conclusion

"So Saul died, and his three sons, and his armourbearer, and all his men, that same day together." (I Samuel 31:6)

"These six things doth the LORD hate: yea, seven are an abomination unto him: . . . he that soweth discord among brethren." (Proverbs 6:16, 19)

Here is the conclusion of the battle in our opening story. It is not just the leader who is harmed by disunity. It was his family, his right hand man and all his men. Disunity destroys men, women, families, friendships and churches. No one escapes unscathed.

On the contrary where there is unity God commands the blessing. That is how the church started and by the grace of God that is how we will finish. No matter what "position" (or no "position") you hold consider yourself to be an armourbearer. You are a person with a high calling. You can labor in prayer. You can labor in fasting. You can labor in fidelity, loyalty, faithfulness. You can labor in love. You can labor to support God's leader. You can protect the unity.

Hopefully reading this book has brought an understanding of the power and responsibility you possess. Use that power wisely and reverently. Be faithful. Be loyal. Be vigilant. Anoint the shield!

References

KJV – King James Version, Public Domain

ASV – American Standard Version, Public Domain

NIV – New International Version, "Scripture taken from the HOLY BIBLE, NEW INTERNATIONAL VERSION®. Copyright © 1973, 1978, 1984 Biblica. Used by permission of Zondervan. All rights reserved. The "NIV" and "New International Version" trademarks are registered in the United States Patent and Trademark Office by Biblica. Use of either trademark requires the permission of Biblica." Zondervan, Grand Rapids, MI.

NASB – New American Standard Bible, "Scripture taken from the NEW AMERICAN STANDARD BIBLE®, Copyright © 1960,1962,1963,1968,1971,1972,1973,1975,1977,1995 by The Lockman Foundation. Used by permission.", The Lockman Foundation, La Habra, CA.

The Message, "Scripture taken from *The Message*. Copyright - 1993, 1994, 1995, 1996, 2000, 2001, 2002. Used by permission of NavPress Publishing Group.", NavPress Publishing Group, Colorado Springs, CO.

Strong's Exhaustive Concordance of the Bible, Hendrickson Publishers, Peabody, MS.

The Mirriam-Webster Thesaurus, Pocket Books, New York, NY.

Shield image, www.xnafusion.com/.../round_shield_preview.png

About the Author

Timothy Wodoslawsky served six years of active duty in the U.S. Navy 1984-1990. During this time God saved and called him to Christian service. He has been actively involved in ministry since 1988. Married in 1995, he and his wife Teresa have two daughters, Story and Valena.

Brother Wodoslawsky served as Pastoral Assistant in both Oakland and Corcoran, California. He was pastor of Christ Apostolic Church in Portage, Pennsylvania for six years. Currently he is pastor of Pinedale Tabernacle, a branch work of Truth Tabernacle in Fresno, California.

Made in the USA
Columbia, SC
05 February 2025

53383273R00035